COMMON CORE
MATH
4 Today
Daily Skill Practice

Grade 1

Erin McCarthy

Carson-Dellosa Publishing, LLC
Greensboro, North Carolina

Credits

Content Editor: Jennifer B. Stith
Copy Editor: Sandra Ogle

Visit *carsondellosa.com* for correlations to Common Core State, national, and Canadian provincial standards.

Carson-Dellosa Publishing, LLC
PO Box 35665
Greensboro, NC 27425 USA
carsondellosa.com

ISBN 978-1-62442-599-8
04-215151151

Table of Contents

Introduction

Common Core Math 4 Today: Daily Skill Practice is a perfect supplement to any classroom math curriculum. Students' math skills will grow as they work on numbers, operations, algebraic thinking, place value, measurement, data, and geometry.

This book covers 40 weeks of daily practice. Four math problems a week will provide students with ample practice in math skills. A separate assessment of five questions is included for the fifth day of each week.

Various skills and concepts are reinforced throughout the book through activities that align to the Common Core State Standards. To view these standards, please see the Common Core State Standards Alignment Matrix on pages 7 and 8.

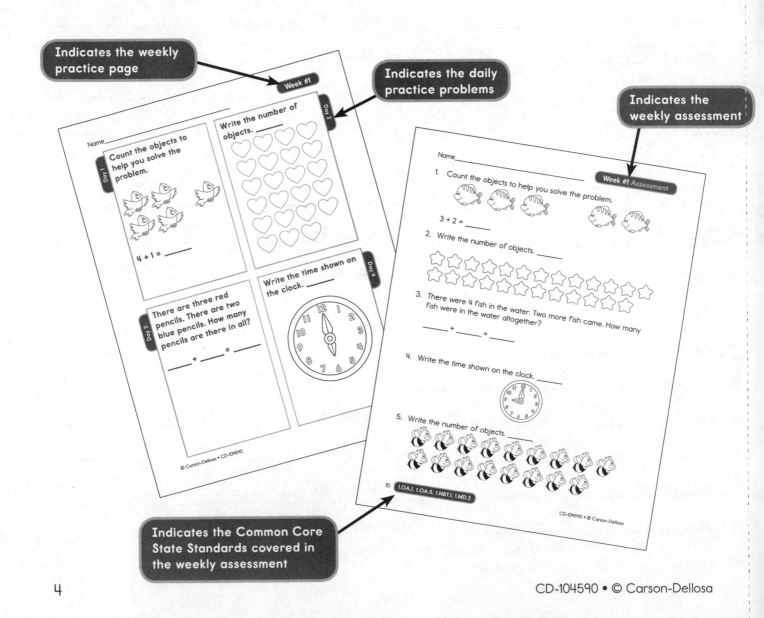

Indicates the weekly practice page

Indicates the daily practice problems

Indicates the weekly assessment

Indicates the Common Core State Standards covered in the weekly assessment

The daily practice problems and weekly assessments in *Common Core Math 4 Today: Daily Skill Practice* help students achieve proficiency with the grade-level Common Core State Standards. Throughout the year, students should also work on building their comfort with the Standards for Mathematical Practice. Use the following suggestions to extend the problems in *Common Core Math 4 Today: Daily Skill Practice*.

1. **Make sense of problems and persevere in solving them.**

   Students should make sure that they understand a problem before trying to solve it. After solving, students should check their answers, often just by asking themselves if their answers make sense in the context of the question. Incorporate the following ideas into your Math 4 Today time:

   • Encourage students to underline the important parts of word problems and to draw lines through any extra information.
   • Allow students to talk through their answers with partners and explain why they think their answers make sense.

2. **Reason abstractly and quantitatively.**

   Students should be able to represent problems with numbers and symbols without losing the original meaning of the numbers and the symbols. A student who is successful at this practice will be able to reason about questions related to the original problem and use flexibility in solving problems. Incorporate the following ideas into your Math 4 Today time:

   • Ask students questions to extend the problems. For example, if a problem asks students to evenly divide a set of 10, ask them to describe what they would do if the set increased to 11.
   • Have students choose a computation problem and write a word problem to accompany it.

3. **Construct viable arguments and critique the reasoning of others.**

   Students should understand mathematical concepts well enough to be able to reason about and prove or disprove answers. As students become more comfortable with mathematical language, they should use math talk to explain their thinking. Incorporate the following ideas into your Math 4 Today time:

   • Have students work with partners and use mathematical language to explain their ways of thinking about a problem.
   • Encourage students to use manipulatives and drawings to support their reasoning.

4. **Model with mathematics.**

   Students should apply their mathematical knowledge to situations in the real world. They can use drawings, graphs, charts, and other tools to make sense of situations, as well as use skills such as estimation to approach a problem before solving it. Incorporate the following ideas into your Math 4 Today time:

- Encourage students to take a problem they have solved and explain how it could help them solve a problem in their own lives.
- Ask students to identify tools, such as charts or graphs, that could help them solve a problem.

5. **Use appropriate tools strategically.**

Students should be able to use a range of tools to help them solve problems, as well as make decisions about which tools to use in different situations. Proficient students will use skills such as estimation to evaluate if the tools helped them solve the problem correctly. Incorporate the following ideas into your Math 4 Today time:

- Ask students to discuss which tools would be most and least helpful in solving a problem.
- As a class, discuss how two students using the same tool could have arrived at the same answer. Encourage students to identify the errors and the limitations in using certain tools.

6. **Attend to precision.**

Students should be thorough in their use of mathematical symbols and labels. They should understand that without them, and without understanding their meanings, math problems are not as meaningful. Incorporate the following ideas into your Math 4 Today time:

- Ask students to explain how a problem or an answer would change if a label on a graph were changed.
- Have students go on a scavenger hunt for the week to identify units of measure in the problems, operations symbols, or graph labels.

7. **Look for and make use of structure.**

Students identify and use patterns to help them extend their knowledge to new concepts. Understanding patterns and structure will also help students be flexible in their approaches to solving problems. Incorporate the following ideas into your Math 4 Today time:

- Have students become pattern detectives and look for any patterns in each week's problems.
- Ask students to substitute a different set of numbers into a problem and see if any patterns emerge.

8. **Look for and express regularity in repeated reasoning.**

Students are able to use any patterns they notice to find shortcuts that help them solve other problems. They can observe a problem with an eye toward finding repetition, instead of straight computation. Incorporate the following ideas into your Math 4 Today time:

- Allow students to share any shortcuts they may find during their problem solving. As a class, try to understand why the shortcuts work.
- When students find patterns, have them explain how the patterns could help them solve other problems.

CD-104590 • © Carson-Dellosa

Common Core State Standards Alignment Matrix

STANDARD	W1	W2	W3	W4	W5	W6	W7	W8	W9	W10	W11	W12	W13	W14	W15	W16	W17	W18	W19	W20
1.OA.1	●		●		●		●		●		●		●				●	●	●	
1.OA.2		●		●	●		●													
1.OA.3												●		●						
1.OA.4											●		●		●		●			
1.OA.5	●		●		●		●		●											
1.OA.6		●		●		●		●		●	●			●		●		●	●	
1.OA.7		●		●		●		●		●		●				●				
1.OA.8		●		●		●		●		●			●		●		●		●	●
1.NBT.1	●				●			●												
1.NBT.2a																				
1.NBT.2b																				
1.NBT.2c																				
1.NBT.3																				
1.NBT.4																				
1.NBT.5																				
1.NBT.6																				
1.MD.1												●		●		●		●		●
1.MD.2											●				●				●	
1.MD.3	●		●			●		●												
1.MD.4			●		●				●											
1.G.1													●				●			
1.G.2																				
1.G.3												●		●		●				●

W = Week

Common Core State Standards Alignment Matrix

STANDARD	W21	W22	W23	W24	W25	W26	W27	W28	W29	W30	W31	W32	W33	W34	W35	W36	W37	W38	W39	W40
1.OA.1	•	•	•	•	•	•	•	•	•	•		•		•		•		•		
1.OA.2											•		•		•		•		•	•
1.OA.3											•				•	•				•
1.OA.4													•						•	
1.OA.5																				
1.OA.6														•	•		•			
1.OA.7																				
1.OA.8											•	•					•		•	
1.NBT.1																				
1.NBT.2a		•	•																	
1.NBT.2b										•										
1.NBT.2c					•		•		•											
1.NBT.3		•	•	•		•		•		•										
1.NBT.4	•		•		•		•		•		•		•		•					
1.NBT.5	•	•		•		•		•		•		•								
1.NBT.6														•		•		•		•
1.MD.1	•					•														
1.MD.2							•					•								•
1.MD.3				•				•							•					
1.MD.4								•				•						•		
1.G.1																				
1.G.2					•											•				
1.G.3																				

W = Week

Name_____

Day 1

Count the objects to help you solve the problem.

4 + 1 = _____

Day 2

Write the number of objects. _____

Day 3

There are three red pencils, There are two blue pencils. How many pencils are there in all?

_____ + _____ = _____

Day 4

Write the time shown on the clock. _____

Name_____

1. Count the objects to help you solve the problem.

3 + 2 = _____

2. Write the number of objects. _____

3. There were 4 fish in the water. Two more fish came. How many fish were in the water altogether?

_____ + _____ = _____

4. Write the time shown on the clock. _____

5. Write the number of objects. _____

1.OA.1, 1.OA.5, 1.NBT.1, 1.MD.3

Day 1

If 7 + 2 = 9,
then 2 + 7 = _____ .

Day 2

Write the number that makes the number sentence true.

10 + _____ = 15

Day 3

Write the word true or false on the line.

_____

1 + 9 = 9 + 1

Day 4

$$\begin{array}{r} 3 \\ + 4 \\ \hline \end{array}$$

1. If 4 + 6 = 10, then 6 + 4 = _____.

2.   7
    + 7
    ‾‾‾

3. Write the word **true** or **false** on the line.

    _____

    4 + 5 = 5 + 4

4. Write the number that makes the number sentence true.

    8 + _____ = 13

5.   8
    + 2
    ‾‾‾

Day 1

Ask 7 classmates which sport they like best. In the table below, make a tally mark beside the sport each one likes best.

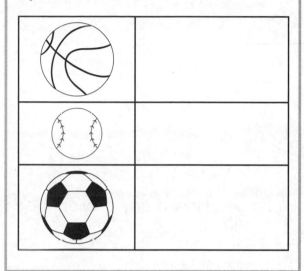

Day 2

Write the time shown on the clock. _____

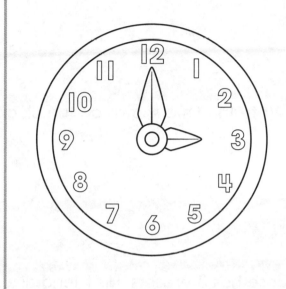

Day 3

Maggie picks 6 flowers. Her mom gives her 2 more flowers. How many flowers does Maggie have?

Maggie has _____ flowers.

Day 4

Count the objects to help you solve the problem.

3 + 3 = _____

Name_____

1. Draw hands on the clock to show 5:00.

2. Write the time shown on the clock. _____

3. Jose has 3 erasers. His friend gives him 1 more. How many erasers does Jose have?

   Jose has _____ erasers.

4. Count the objects to help you solve the problem.

   6 + 0 = _____

5. Sally picks 2 flowers. She picks 2 more flowers. How many flowers does she have in all?

   Sally has _____ flowers.

Day 1

Write the number that makes the number sentence true.

_____ + 7 = 15

Day 2

Tyrone caught 11 fish one day. The next day, he caught 9 more fish. How many fish did Tyrone catch in all?

Tyrone caught _____ fish.

Day 3

If 8 + 7 = 15, then 7 + 8 = _____ .

Day 4

Write the word true or false on the line.

_____

7 + 3 = 4 + 7

1. If 5 + 10 = 15, then 10 + 5 = _____.

2. A gardener planted 7 trees in one row. He planted 12 trees in another row. How many trees did he plant in all?

    The gardener planted _____ trees in all.

3. Write the word **true** or **false** on the line.

    _____

    11 + 8 = 9 + 11

4. Write the number that makes the number sentence true.

    _____ + 5 = 7

5. Write the word **true** or **false** on the line.

    _____

    7 + 8 = 8 + 7

Name_____

Day 1

Write the number for each number word.

ten _____

six _____

twelve _____

Day 2

Jan had 4 dolls. Two were lost. How many dolls does Jan have left?

_____ - _____ = _____

Jan has _____ dolls left.

Day 3

```
  8
  9
+ 1
___
```

Day 4

Count the objects to help you solve the problem.

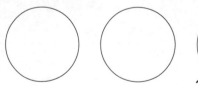

_____ - _____ = _____

Name_____

1. Write the number for each number word.

    eleven _____   three _____   nine _____

2. Five lights were on in the house. James turned off 3 lights. How many lights are still on in the house?

    _____ - _____ = _____

    There are _____ lights still on in the house.

3.   6
      5
    + 2
    ___

4. Count the objects to help you solve the problem.

    _____ - _____ = _____

5.   4
      4
    + 5
    ___

1.OA.1, 1.OA.2, 1.OA.5, 1.NBT.1   CD-104590 • © Carson-Dellosa

Day 1

$$8 \qquad\qquad 5$$
$$-\ 6 \qquad\quad\ -\ 2$$

Day 2

Write the word true
or false on the line.

_____

10 + 8 = 8 + 10

Day 3

Write the number that
makes the number
sentence true.

_____ – 6 = 3

Day 4

Ask 10 classmates which
drink they like best. In
the table below, make
a tally mark beside the
drink each one likes best.

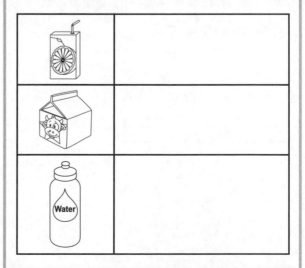

1. $\begin{array}{r} 11 \\ -\ 7 \\ \hline \end{array}$ $\begin{array}{r} 13 \\ -\ 3 \\ \hline \end{array}$

2. Write the word **true** or **false** on the line.

    _____

    $3 + 9 = 3 + 8$

3. Write the number that makes the number sentence true.

    _____ $- 3 = 8$

4. Write the word **true** or **false** on the line.

    _____

    $5 + 2 = 2 + 5$

5. $\begin{array}{r} 9 \\ -\ 5 \\ \hline \end{array}$ $\begin{array}{r} 6 \\ -\ 4 \\ \hline \end{array}$

Day 1

Write the time shown on the clock. _____

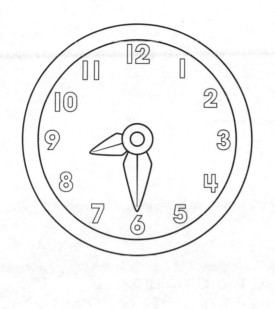

Day 2

If 8 + 8 + 2 = 18, then
8 + 2 + 8 = _____.

Day 3

Count the objects to help you solve the problem.

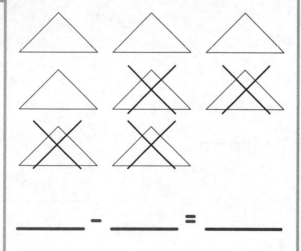

____ - ____ = ____

Day 4

Dante has 9 apples. He gives away 3 apples. How many apples does Dante have left?

____ - ____ = ____

1. Mischa has 11 dolls. She gave 2 dolls to her granddaughter. How many dolls does Mischa have left?

    _____ - _____ = _____

    Mischa has _____ dolls left.

2. If 3 + 6 + 2 = 11, then 6 + 2 + 3 = _____.

3. Count the objects to help you solve the problem.

    _____ - _____ = _____

4. If 9 + 8 + 1 = 18, then 8 + 1 + 9 = _____.

5. Write the time shown on the clock. _____

1.OA.1, 1.OA.2, 1.OA.5, 1.MD.3

CD-104590 • © Carson-Dellosa

Day 1

$$12 \qquad\qquad 7$$
$$-\ 9 \qquad\qquad -\ 5$$

Day 2

Draw a line to match each number word to its number.

twenty-eight   14

fourteen   5

five   28

Day 3

Write the number that makes the number sentence true.

_____ − 5 = 8

Day 4

Write the word true or false on the line.

_____

9 − 3 = 8 − 2

1.   10   12
        − 3   − 4
        ‾‾‾‾   ‾‾‾‾

2. Write the word **true** or **false** on the line.

    _____

    $12 - 7 = 11 - 6$

3. Write the number that makes the number sentence true.

    $8 - $ _____ $= 4$

4. Draw a line to match each number word to its number.

    sixteen   16

    four   20

    twenty   4

5. Write the number that makes the number sentence true.

    $7 - $ _____ $= 1$

Day 1

Nassim wrote 10 emails on Monday. He wrote 6 more emails on Tuesday. How many total emails did Nassim write on Monday and Tuesday?

Nassim wrote _____ total emails on Monday and Tuesday.

Day 2

$$\begin{array}{r} 7 \\ 8 \\ + 3 \\ \hline \end{array}$$

Day 3

Leslie buys 12 gallons of lemonade for the party. She serves 9 gallons of lemonade during the party. How many gallons of lemonade does Leslie have left?

Leslie has _____ gallons of lemonade left.

Day 4

Write the time shown on the clock. _____

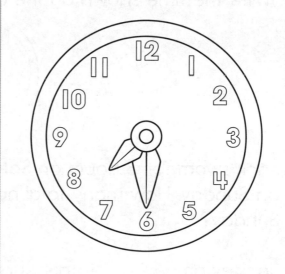

Name_____

1.   2
       2
    + 8
    ____

2. Leo bought 15 stamps. He used 10 stamps. How many stamps does Leo have left?

    Leo has _____ stamps left.

3.   8
       4
    + 4
    ____

4. Write the time shown on the clock. _____

5. Jack swam for 3 hours on Saturday. He swam for 4 more hours on Sunday. How many total hours did Jack swim on Saturday and Sunday?

    Jack swam _____ total hours on Saturday and Sunday.

1.OA.1, 1.OA.5, 1.MD.3   CD-104590 • © Carson-Dellosa

Day 1

Ask 10 classmates what their favorite things to do on the playground are. In the table below, make a tally mark beside the thing each one likes best.

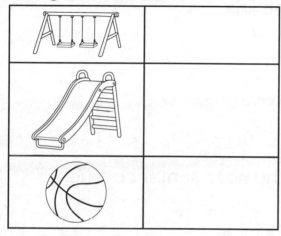

Day 2

$$8$$
$$+ 8$$

$$7$$
$$+ 1$$

Day 3

Write the word true or false on the line.

_____

5 − 4 = 7 − 6

Day 4

Write the number that makes the number sentence true.

9 + _____ = 16

1. Write the number that makes the number sentence true.

_____ – 6 = 4

2. Write the word **true** or **false** on the line.

_____

9 – 1 = 12 – 4

3. Write the number that makes the number sentence true.

_____ – 8 = 3

4.　　11　　　　　　9
　　+ 4　　　　　+ 4
　　———　　　　———

5. Write the word **true** or **false** on the line.

_____

12 – 5 = 10 – 3

Day 1

6 – 2 = 2 + _____

Day 2

Scott picks 11 apples.
He picks 3 more apples.
How many apples does
Scott pick in all?

Scott picks _____
apples in all.

Day 3

$$\begin{array}{r} 15 \\ -\ 8 \\ \hline \end{array}$$ $$\begin{array}{r} 14 \\ -\ 4 \\ \hline \end{array}$$

Day 4

How many cubes long is
the pencil?

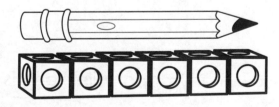

The pencil is _____
cubes long.

1. $9 - 6 = 2 +$ _____

2. How many paper clips long is the screwdriver?

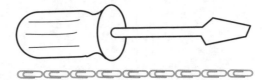

The screwdriver is _____ paper clips long.

3. Brady sees 7 fish in the pond. He sees 9 more fish. How many fish does Brady see in the pond in all?

Brady sees _____ fish in the pond in all.

4. $\begin{array}{r} 16 \\ -\ 9 \\ \hline \end{array}$ $\begin{array}{r} 19 \\ -\ 15 \\ \hline \end{array}$

5. How many paper clips long is the comb?

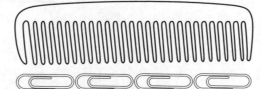

The comb is _____ paper clips long.

Day 1

Number the objects as follows:
1 = long
2 = medium
3 = short

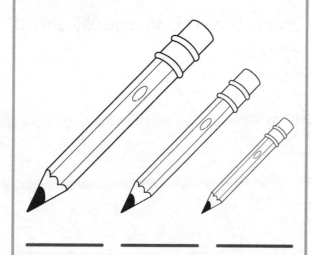

_____   _____   _____

Day 2

Write the word true or false on the line.

_____

9 – 7 = 8 – 6

Day 3

If 5 + 3 = 8,
then 3 + 5 = _____.

Day 4

Draw lines to show how you and a friend can equally share this candy bar.

1. Number the objects as follows: 1 = long; 2 = medium; 3 = short.

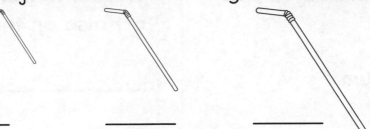

_____   _____   _____

2. Draw lines to show how can you and a friend can equally share this pizza.

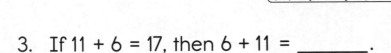

3. If 11 + 6 = 17, then 6 + 11 = _____.

4. Write the word **true** or **false** on the line.

    _____

    13 – 4 = 9 – 5

5. If 8 + 3 = 11, then 3 + 8 = _____.

Day 1

Circle the square.

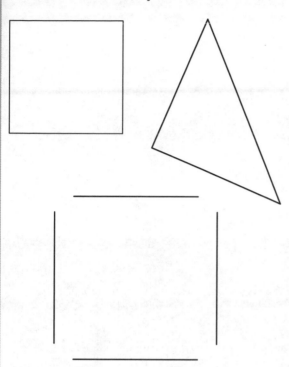

Day 2

Write the number that makes the number sentence true.

_____ + 5 = 19

Day 3

Fifteen birds are in a tree. Nine fly away. How many birds are left in the end?

_____ birds are left in the end.

Day 4

8 – 2 = 2 + _____

1. Mia picked 10 tomatoes. She gave 3 to her neighbor. How many tomatoes does Mia have left?

    Mia has _____ tomatoes left.

2. $7 - 4 = 2 +$ _____

3. Draw a square.

4. Mrs. Freeman bakes 16 cupcakes. She sells 4. How many cupcakes does Mrs. Freeman have left?

    Mrs. Freeman has _____ cupcakes left.

5. Write the number that makes the number sentence true.

    _____ $+ 1 = 18$

1.OA.1, 1.OA.4, 1.OA.8, 1.G.1

Day 1

$$\begin{array}{r} 15 \\ + 3 \\ \hline \end{array} \qquad \begin{array}{r} 6 \\ + 5 \\ \hline \end{array}$$

Day 2

Number the objects as follows:

1 = long

2 = medium

3 = short

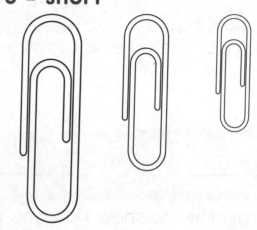

_____ _____ _____

Day 3

Draw lines to show how you and 3 friends can equally share this graham cracker.

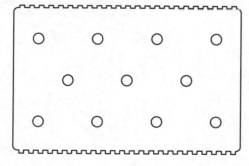

Day 4

$$\begin{array}{r} 4 \\ 7 \\ + 2 \\ \hline \end{array}$$

1.
```
   6
   1
 + 9
-----
```

2. Number the objects as follows: 1 = long; 2 = medium; 3 = short.

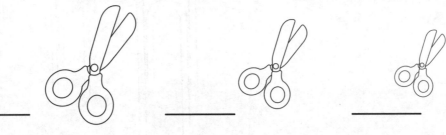

_____   _____   _____

3. Draw lines to show how you and 3 friends can equally share this brownie.

4.
```
   1
   2
 + 4
-----
```

5.
```
   2            6
 + 6          + 6
-----        -----
```

Name_____

Day 1

Write the number that makes the number sentence true.

12 – _____ = 7

Day 2

12 – 9 = 2 + _____

Day 3

How many fish long is the fishing rod?

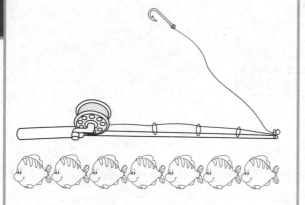

The fishing rod is _____ fish long.

Day 4

We saw 16 dolphins playing in the water. We saw 3 swim away. How many dolphins are left playing in the water?

_____ dolphins are left playing in the water.

1. Write the number that makes the number sentence true.

    5 – _____ = 1

2. There are 7 first graders playing on the playground. Three leave to play in the sandbox. How many students are left playing on the playground?

    _____ students are left playing on the playground.

3. 10 – 5 = 4 + _____

4. How many cubes long is the spoon?

    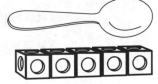

    The spoon is _____ cubes long.

5. Seventeen fish are in the coral. Eight swim away. How many fish are left in the coral?

    _____ fish are left in the coral.

Day 1

Write the word true or false on the line.

_____

$10 + 3 = 3 + 4$

Day 2

Draw a line to show how you and 1 friend can equally share this cookie.

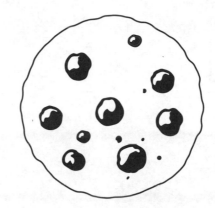

Day 3

Number the objects as follows:
1 = long
2 = medium
3 = short

_____   _____   _____

Day 4

$$\begin{array}{r} 9 \\ -\ 6 \\ \hline \end{array} \qquad \begin{array}{r} 11 \\ -\ 3 \\ \hline \end{array}$$

1. Write the word **true** or **false** on the line.

   _____

   $5 + 6 = 2 + 9$

2. $\begin{array}{r} 1 \\ + 8 \\ \hline \end{array}$ $\begin{array}{r} 6 \\ + 3 \\ \hline \end{array}$

3. Number the objects as follows: 1 = long; 2 = medium; 3 = short.

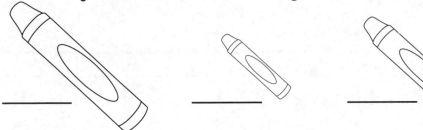

   _____   _____   _____

4. Draw a line to show how you and 1 friend can equally share this apple pie.

5. $\begin{array}{r} 4 \\ - 4 \\ \hline \end{array}$ $\begin{array}{r} 3 \\ - 2 \\ \hline \end{array}$

1.OA.6, 1.OA.7, 1.MD.1, 1.G.3

Day 1

Claire ate 1 banana for breakfast. She ate 7 grapes for snack. How many pieces of fruit did she eat in all?

Claire ate _____ pieces of fruit in all.

Day 2

Circle the rectangle.

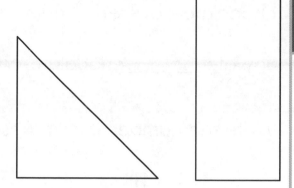

Day 3

11 – 4 = 4 + _____

Day 4

Write the number that makes the number sentence true.

_____ + 7 = 14

1. Jay ate 11 pieces of chocolate-covered candies yesterday. Today, he ate 7 pieces of chocolate-covered candies. How many chocolate-covered candies did Jay eat in all?

   Jay ate _____ chocolate-covered candies in all.

2. Write the number that makes the number sentence true.

   _____ + 7 = 11

3. 8 – 3 = 3 + _____

4. Draw a rectangle.

5. 12 – 3 = 3 + _____

1.OA.1, 1.OA.4, 1.OA.8, 1.G.1

Day 1

Tia counted 10 blossoms on the plant. Three fell off. How many blossoms are left on the plant?

_____ blossoms are left on the plant.

Day 2

I watched 20 sharks race in the water. I watched 6 stop to watch fish. How many sharks are still racing?

_____ sharks are still racing.

Day 3

$$8 + 6$$ $$4 - 2$$

Day 4

Number the objects as follows:
1 = long
2 = medium
3 = short

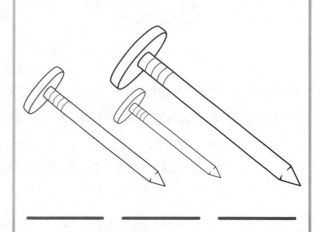

_____ _____ _____

1. A total of 18 jellyfish swam around a sunken ship. A group of 12 swam into the ship. How many jellyfish are still swimming around the ship?

   _____jellyfish are still swimming around the ship.

2. $\begin{array}{r} 4 \\ + 4 \\ \hline \end{array}$ $\qquad$ $\begin{array}{r} 7 \\ - 5 \\ \hline \end{array}$

3. Yasmin's aunt gave her 13 stickers to decorate her notebook. Yasmin gave 9 of the stickers to her best friend. How many stickers does Yasmin have left?

   Yasmin has _____ stickers left.

4. Number the objects as follows: 1 = long; 2 = medium; 3 = short.

5. Farmer Evan planted 14 pumpkin seeds. Birds ate 4 seeds. How many pumpkin seeds are left?

   _____ pumpkin seeds are left.

Day 1

Blake has 10 hats. He gives away 4 hats. How many hats does Blake have left?

Blake has _____ hats left.

Day 2

$$\begin{array}{r} 5 \\ + 4 \\ \hline \end{array} \qquad \begin{array}{r} 10 \\ + 9 \\ \hline \end{array}$$

Day 3

Write the number that makes the number sentence true.

_____ + 3 = 14

Day 4

How many fish tall is the fisherman?

The fisherman is _____ fish tall.

1. How many fish long is the boat?

The boat is _____ fish long.

2.   14   16
    + 2   + 3
    ____   ____

3. Write the number that makes the number sentence true.

    _____ + 10 = 18

4.   12   10
    + 4   + 2
    ____   ____

5. Olivia had 15 towels for the pool party. Eight towels were used. How many towels were not used?

    _____ towels were not used.

Day 1

Number the objects as follows:

1 = long
2 = medium
3 = short

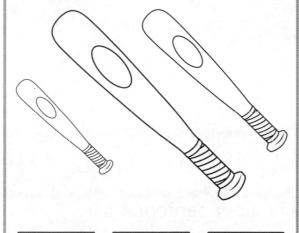

____ ____ ____

Day 2

Write the word true or false on the line.

_____

$5 + 9 = 7 + 7$

Day 3

Write the number that makes the number sentence true.

$10 - \underline{\hspace{1cm}} = 7$

Day 4

Draw lines to show how you and 3 friends can equally share this cake.

Name_____

1. Draw lines to show how you and 3 friends can equally share this pizza.

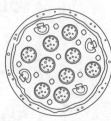

2. Write the word **true** or **false** on the line.

_____

$7 + 5 = 4 + 8$

3. Write the number that makes the number sentence true.

$8 - \underline{\hspace{1.5cm}} = 3$

4. Write the word **true** or **false** on the line.

_____

$6 + 7 = 9 + 6$

5. Number the objects as follows: 1 = long; 2 = medium; 3 = short.

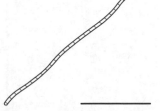

_____   _____   _____

Day 1

Ana typed for 7 hours. She typed for 5 more hours later. How many hours did Ana type in all?

Ana typed for _____ hours in all.

Day 2

15
+ 3
_____

Day 3

Write the number that is 10 more than the number shown.

19 _____

Day 4

Number the objects as follows:
1 = long
2 = medium
3 = short

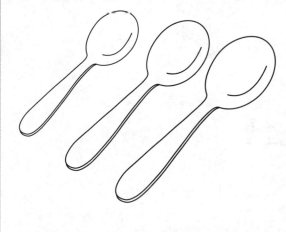

_____ _____ _____

1. Corinna has 4 cousins on her mom's side. She has 7 cousins on her dad's side. How many cousins does Corinna have in all?

    Corinna has _____ cousins in all.

2. $\begin{array}{r} 11 \\ + 2 \\ \hline \end{array}$

3. Write the number that is 10 more than the number shown.

    28 _____

4. Number the objects as follows: 1 = long; 2 = medium; 3 = short.

    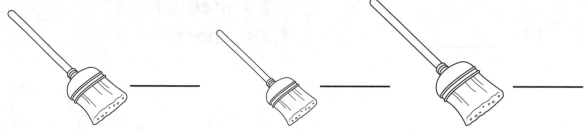

    _____   _____   _____

5. $\begin{array}{r} 27 \\ + 6 \\ \hline \end{array}$

1.OA.1, 1.NBT.4, 1.NBT.5, 1.MD.1

Day 1

Circle each set of 10 objects. Write the total amount of tens and ones.

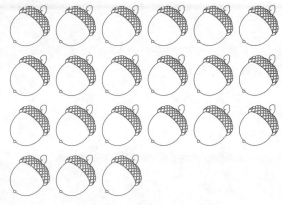

_____ tens _____ one

Day 2

Write <, >, or = to make the statement true.

40 ◯ 37

Day 3

Jarvis worked on an art project for 14 days. Brian worked on the same art project for 11 days. How many more days did Jarvis work on the art project than Brian?

Jarvis worked _____ more days on the art project than Brian.

Day 4

Write the number that is 10 less than the number shown.

16 _____

1. Write the number that is 10 less than the number shown.

   86   _____

2. Write <, >, or = to make the statement true.

   55 ◯ 35

3. April orders 8 sandwiches. Five of the sandwiches are turkey. How many of the sandwiches are not turkey?

   _____ of the sandwiches are not turkey.

4. Write the number that is 10 less than the number shown.

   26   _____

5. Circle each set of 10 objects. Write the total amount of tens and ones.

   _____ ten _____ ones

1.OA.1, 1.NBT.2, 1.NBT.3, 1.NBT.5   CD-104590 • © Carson-Dellosa

Day 1

Lauren stamped 9 letters. She stamped 7 more letters later. How many letters did Lauren stamp in all?

Lauren stamped _____ letters in all.

Day 2

Circle each set of 10 objects. Write the total amount of tens and ones.

_____ tens _____ ones

Day 3

Write <, >, or = to make the statement true.

22 ◯ 44

Day 4

24
+ 5
―――

1. Circle each set of 10 objects. Write the total amount of tens and ones.

_____ ten _____ ones

2. Write <, >, or = to make the statement true.

14 ◯ 32

3. Spot chewed 6 bones in the morning. He chewed 9 bones in the afternoon. How many bones did Spot chew in all?

Spot chewed _____ bones in all.

4. 19
    + 6
    ____

5. Write <, >, or = to make the statement true.

75 ◯ 95

Day 1

Write the time shown on the clock. _____

Day 2

Write the number that is 10 less than the number shown.

52 _____

Day 3

Bill sells 12 newspapers in one day. He sells 6 newspapers the next day. How many more newspapers did Bill sell on the first day?

Bill sold _____ more newspapers on the first day.

Day 4

Write <, >, or = to make the statement true.

59 ◯ 39

1. Write the number that is 10 less than the number shown.

   61   _____

2. Shannon received 18 phone calls last Wednesday. She received only 5 phone calls last Thursday. How many more phone calls did Shannon receive on Wednesday?

   Shannon received _____ more phone calls on Wednesday.

3. Sixteen friends were at Ella's party. Thirteen of the friends ate cake. How many friends did not eat cake?

   _____ friends did not eat cake.

4. Write <, >, or = to make the statement true.

   52 ◯ 21

5. Write the time shown on the clock. _____

Day 1

Eleven trees are in Greg's yard. Five of the trees have flowers. The rest do not. How many of the trees do not have flowers?

_____ of the trees do not have flowers.

Day 2

54
+ 3
___

Day 3

Circle the triangle.

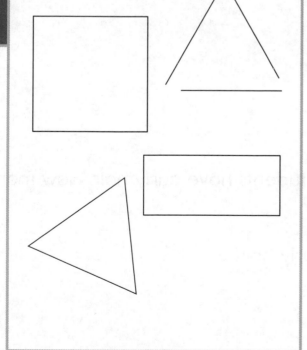

Day 4

Write the value of the number.

60

_____ tens

_____ ones

1.
$$\begin{array}{r} 61 \\ + 8 \\ \hline \end{array}$$

2. Draw a triangle.

3. Write the value of the number.

   30

   _____ tens   _____ ones

4.
$$\begin{array}{r} 65 \\ + 4 \\ \hline \end{array}$$

5. Out of a class of 18 students, 7 students have curly hair. How many students do not have curly hair?

   _____ students do not have curly hair.

1.OA.1, 1.NBT.2, 1.NBT.4, 1.G.2

Day 1

Number the objects as follows:
1 = long
2 = medium
3 = short

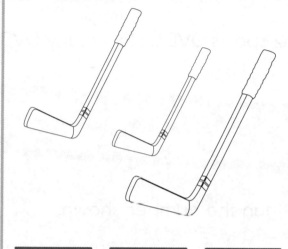

_____ _____ _____

Day 2

Write <, >, or = to make the statement true.

56 ◯ 26

Day 3

Sara inflates 17 blue balloons. She inflates 3 more red balloons. How many balloons does Sara inflate in all?

Sara inflates _____ balloons in all.

Day 4

Write the number that is 10 less than the number shown.

39 _____

1. Write <, >, or = to make the statement true.

17  30

2. Seth has 5 comedy DVDs. He has 2 sports DVDs. How many DVDs does Seth have in all?

Seth has _____ DVDs in all.

3. Write the number that is 10 more than the number shown.

23 _____

4. Number the objects as follows: 1 = long; 2 = medium; 3 = short.

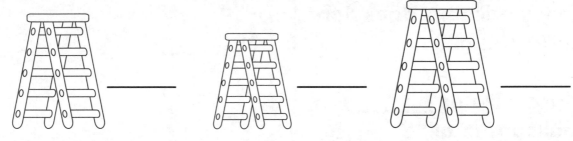

5. Write <, >, or = to make the statement true.

61  31

Name_____

Day 1

Pedro hit 2 home runs on Saturday. He hit 5 home runs on Sunday. How many more home runs did Pedro hit on Sunday?

Pedro hit _____ more home runs on Sunday.

Day 2

Write the value of the number.

80

_____ tens

_____ ones

Day 3

How many cubes long is the toothbrush?

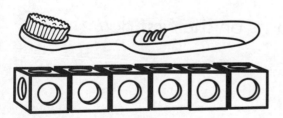

The toothbrush is _____ cubes long.

Day 4

$$\begin{array}{r} 44 \\ + 6 \\ \hline \end{array}$$

1. Emma bought 12 eggs at the grocery store. Eight eggs broke on the way home from the store. How many eggs does Emma have left?

   Emma has _____ eggs left.

2. How many cubes long is the fork?

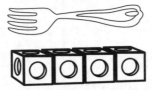

   The fork is _____ cubes long.

3.   33
    + 7
    _____

4. Mason sold 19 candy bars on the first day. He sold 7 candy bars on the second day. How many more candy bars did Mason sell on the first day?

   Mason sold _____ more candy bars on the first day.

5. Write the value of the number.

   40

   _____ tens   _____ ones

1.OA.1, 1.NBT.2, 1.NBT.4, 1.MD.2

Day 1

Write the time shown on the clock. _____

Day 2

Write the number that is 10 less than the number shown.

65 _____

Day 3

Miranda orders 17 scarves. Twelve scarves come in the mail on Monday. How many more scarves still need to come?

_____ more scarves still need to come.

Day 4

Write <, >, or = to make the statement true.

27 ◯ 38

1. Uma has 20 baseball cards. She gives away 11 cards. How many cards does Uma have left?

   Uma has _____ cards left.

2. 52 + 20 = _____

3. Write <, >, or = to make the statement true.

   28 ◯ 38

4. Write the time shown on the clock. _____

5. Write the number that is 10 more than the number shown.

   41   _____

1.OA.1, 1.NBT.3, 1.NBT.5, 1.MD.3

Day 1

Sam hangs 10 pictures one day. She hangs 8 pictures the next day. How many pictures does Sam hang in all?

Sam hangs _____ pictures in all.

Day 2

18 + 70 = _____

Day 3

Look at the tally chart. How many more people like purple best than like orange best?

Favorite Colors		
Orange	Purple	Yellow

_____ more people like purple best.

Day 4

Write the value of the number.

90

_____ tens

_____ ones

1. Look at the tally chart. What color of hair do more people have?

   More people have _____ hair.

Hair Color		
Brown	Black	Blonde
ⵌ III	ⵌ I	III

2. Write the value of the number.

   50

   _____ tens   _____ ones

3. Write the value of the number.

   70

   _____ tens   _____ ones

4. Kennedy collects ladybugs. She collected 13 ladybugs in one jar. She collected 5 ladybugs in another jar. How many ladybugs did Kennedy collect in all?

   Kennedy collected _____ ladybugs in all.

5. 25 + 70 = _____

Day 1

Write the value of the number.

15

_____ ten

_____ ones

Day 2

Write <, >, or = to make the statement true.

73 ◯ 53

Day 3

Juan has 12 papers in his folder. He gives 7 papers to his teacher. How many papers does Juan have left in his folder?

Juan has _____ papers left in his folder.

Day 4

Write the number that is 10 more than the number shown.

63 _____

1. Melissa drew 16 triangles. She colored 5 triangles orange. She left the rest of the triangles white. How many triangles did Melissa leave white?

   Melissa left _____ triangles white.

2. Write the number that is 10 more than the number shown.

   43   _____

3. Write the value of the number.

   11

   _____ ten _____ one

4. Kasey bought 19 palm trees. She planted 8 palm trees in her front yard. How many palm trees does Kasey have left to plant in her backyard?

   Kasey has _____ palm trees left to plant in her backyard.

5. Write <, >, or = to make the statement true.

   89 ◯ 83

Day 1

Write the number that makes the number sentence true.

11 + _____ = 16

Day 2

Anna had 6 marbles. Brad had 6 marbles. Chelsea had 4 marbles. How many marbles did Anna, Brad, and Chelsea have altogether?

_____ + _____ + _____ = _____

Anna, Brad, and Chelsea had _____ marbles altogether.

Day 3

$$\begin{array}{r} 51 \\ + 8 \\ \hline \end{array}$$

Day 4

If 9 – 7 = 2, then 9 – 2 = _____ .

1. Dion swam 7 laps in the pool in the morning. He swam 4 more laps after lunch. He took a 20-minute break and swam 2 more laps. How many laps did Dion swim in all?

    _____ + _____ + _____ = _____   Dion swam _____ laps in all.

2. If 11 – 3 = 8, then 11 – 8 = _____.

3. Write the number that makes the number sentence true.

    5 + _____ = 7

4.   29
       + 3
      ____

5. Reese makes 5 phone calls on Saturday. He makes 4 phone calls on Sunday. Reese makes 1 more phone call on Monday. How many phone calls total did Reese make on Saturday, Sunday, and Monday?

    _____ + _____ + _____ = _____

    Reese made _____ phone calls total on Saturday, Sunday, and Monday.

1.OA.2, 1.OA.3, 1.OA.8, 1.NBT.4   CD-104590 • © Carson-Dellosa

Day 1

Look at the tally chart. Who has the most pennies in her piggy bank?

Pennies in the Piggy Bank		
Alexa	Grace	Lynn
卌 卌 卌	卌 卌	卌 丨丨丨丨 卌

_____ has the most pennies in her piggy bank.

Day 2

Tony is reading a book that has 20 pages. He has read 10 pages. How many pages does Tony have left to read?

Tony has _____ pages left to read.

Day 3

How many tennis balls tall is the tennis racket?

The tennis racket is _____ tennis balls tall.

Day 4

Write the number that makes the number sentence true.

_____ – 2 = 14

1. Look at the tally chart. How many more snowy days were there in January than in March?

    _____ more snowy days were in January than in March.

Snowy Days		
January	February	March
卌 卌 |||	卌 卌	卌 |||

2. Oliver buys 16 T-shirts at the ball game. He gives away 8 T-shirts. How many T-shirts does he have left?

    Oliver has _____ T-shirts left.

3. How many buttons tall is the notepad?

    The notepad is _____ buttons tall.

4. Write the number that makes the number sentence true.

    _____ – 7 = 9

5. Look at the tally chart. How many more blue cars were on the road than red cars?

Cars on the Road		
Blue	Red	White

    _____ more blue cars were on the road than red cars.

Day 1

14 + 40 = _____

Day 2

Ellen, Fiona, and Gene have 5 pet fish each. How many pet fish do they have altogether?

_____ + _____ + _____ =

_____

Ellen, Fiona, and Gene have _____ pet fish altogether.

Day 3

17 – 3 = 3 + _____

Day 4

Write the number that is 10 more than the number shown.

74 _____

1. Xander played 3 computer games one week. He played 7 computer games the next week. He played 0 computer games the third week. How many computer games did Xander play in all?

    _____ + _____ + _____ = _____

    Xander played _____ computer games in all.

2. 66 + 20 = _____

3. 19 – 14 = 4 + _____

4. Jonathan read 7 pages of his book last night. He read 2 more pages this morning. When he got to school, he read 6 more pages. How many pages did Jonathan read in all?

    _____ + _____ + _____ = _____

    Jonathan read _____ pages in all.

5. Write the number that is 10 more than the number shown.

    72   _____

Day 1

13
+ 3
_____

7
+ 3
_____

Day 2

Write the time shown on the clock. _____

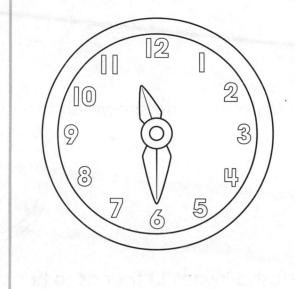

Day 3

Lucy has some marbles in her pocket. Eight of the marbles in her pocket are red. The other 12 marbles in her pocket are black. How many marbles does Lucy have in all?

Lucy has _____ marbles in all.

Day 4

69
+ 4
_____

1. 37
    + 3
    ———

2. Write the time shown on the clock. _____

3. Tasha invites 13 friends to her slumber party. Two of her friends cannot come to the party. How many friends are able to come to Tasha's slumber party?

    _____ friends are able to come to Tasha's slumber party.

4.   2   9
    + 8   + 10
    ———   ———

5. Write the time shown on the clock. _____

1.OA.1, 1.OA.6, 1.NBT.6, 1.MD.3

Day 1

$$9 - 3$$

$$11 - 9$$

Day 2

57 + 30 = _____

Day 3

Molly ate 4 cherries, 8 grapes, and 1 orange for breakfast. How many pieces of fruit did Molly eat in all?

_____ + _____ + _____ =

_____

Molly ate _____ pieces of fruit in all.

Day 4

If 13 – 5 = 8, then 13 – 8 = _____.

Name_____

1. 28 + 60 =

2.   13   8
      – 7   – 2
      ___   ___

3. Owen ate 1 potato, 6 green beans, and 5 baby carrots for dinner. How many vegetables did Owen eat in all?

    _____ + _____ + _____ = _____

    Owen ate _____ vegetables in all.

4. If 12 – 5 = 7, then 12 – 7 = _____.

5. Zane has 2 baseball cards. Chang gives him 5 more. Zane finds 1 more baseball card in his desk. How many baseball cards does Zane have in all?

    _____ + _____ + _____ = _____

    Zane has _____ baseball cards in all.

1.OA.2, 1.OA.3, 1.OA.6, 1.NBT.4   CD-104590 • © Carson-Dellosa

Day 1

If 4 + 9 = 13,
then 9 + 4 = _____ .

Day 2

Circle the trapezoid.

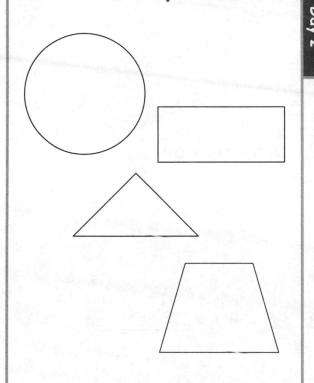

Day 3

Veronica has 6 brothers.
She also has 5 sisters.
How many brothers and
sisters does Veronica
have in all?

Veronica has _____
brothers and sisters
in all.

Day 4

80 – 70 =

1. 90 – 90 = _____

2. Draw a trapezoid.

3. 90 – 40 = _____

4. Wendy ran 5 miles on Tuesday. She ran 3 miles on Thursday. How many total miles did Wendy run on Tuesday and Thursday?

    Wendy ran _____ total miles on Tuesday and Thursday.

5. If 15 + 2 = 17, then 2 + 15 = _____ .

1.OA.1, 1.OA.3, 1.NBT.6, 1.G.2

Day 1

$$14 \qquad\qquad 9$$
$$\underline{-\ 7} \qquad\quad \underline{-\ 9}$$

Day 2

Write the number that is 10 less than the number shown.

88 _____

Day 3

Write the number that makes the number sentence true.

_____ + 10 = 17

Day 4

On Monday and Tuesday, Quan drank 3 glasses of water each day. On Wednesday, he drank 5 glasses of water. How many glasses of water did Quan drink in all?

_____ + _____ + _____ =

_____

Quan drank _____ glasses of water in all.

1. At the pet store, 6 hamsters, 7 fish, and 2 lizards are for sale. How many pets are for sale at the pet store?

    _____ + _____ + _____ = _____

    _____ pets are for sale at the pet store.

2. Write the number that makes the number sentence true.

    _____ + 3 = 15

3. Write the number that is 10 less than the number shown.

    29   _____

4. Mrs. Avery bought 5 boxes of pasta, 3 bananas, and 9 muffins at the grocery store. How many food items did Mrs. Avery buy in all?

    _____ + _____ + _____ = _____

    Mrs. Avery bought _____ food items in all.

5.
    $$\begin{array}{r} 15 \\ + 3 \\ \hline \end{array} \qquad \begin{array}{r} 4 \\ - 2 \\ \hline \end{array}$$

Day 1

Uma has 17 hamsters. She gave 3 to her friends. How many hamsters does Uma have left?

Uma has _____ hamsters left.

Day 2

Look at the tally chart. How many more children like pepperoni pizza than mushroom pizza?

Favorite Pizza		
Pepperoni	Mushroom	Cheese
IIII	II	III

_____ more children like pepperoni pizza.

Day 3

Write the number that is 10 more than the number shown.

51 _____

Day 4

50 − 50 = _____

Name_____

1. Look at the tally chart. How many more medium-sized dogs than large dogs live on Hay Street?

Dogs on Hay Street		
Small	Medium	Large
卌	卌	|||

_____ more medium-sized dogs than large dogs live on Hay Street.

2. 70 – 20 = _____

3. Fifteen umbrellas are by the front door. Seven of the umbrellas are red. The rest are yellow. How many of the umbrellas are yellow?

_____ of the umbrellas are yellow.

4. 30 – 20 = _____

5. Write the number that is 10 more than the number shown.

49   _____

1.OA.1, 1.NBT.6, 1.MD.4   CD-104590 • © Carson-Dellosa

Day 1

Heath bought 8 pencils, 7 erasers, and 2 notebooks for school. How many school supplies did Heath buy?

_____ + _____ + _____ =

_____

Heath bought _____ school supplies.

Day 2

19 – 9 = 9 + _____

Day 3

Write the number that makes the number sentence true.

_____ + 9 = 15

Day 4

Write the number that is 10 less than the number shown.

78   _____

1. Six ducks, 3 frogs, and 1 swan are swimming in the pond. How many animals are swimming in the pond in all?

   _____ + _____ + _____ = _____

   _____ animals are swimming in the pond in all.

2. Write the number that makes the number sentence true.

   _____ + 7 = 10

3. Write the number that is 10 less than the number shown.

   50   _____

4. 15 – 11 = 1 + _____

5. Ivan bought 3 packs of baseball cards. Each pack has 4 cards. How many cards does Ivan have in all?

   _____ + _____ + _____ = _____

   Ivan has _____ baseball cards in all.

1.OA.2, 1.OA.4, 1.OA.8

Day 1

70 – 20 = _____

Day 2

Yolanda baked 7 chocolate chip cookies, 5 peanut butter cookies, and 3 oatmeal cookies. How many cookies did Yolanda bake in all?

_____ + _____ + _____ = _____

Yolanda baked _____ cookies in all.

Day 3

How many nails long is the hammer?

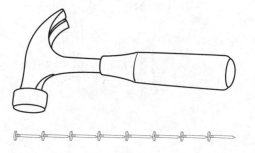

The hammer is _____ nails long.

Day 4

If 13 + 3 = 16,
then 3 + 13 = _____.

1. If 18 + 2 = 20, then 2 + 18 = _____ .

2. 60 – 60 = _____

3. Riley has 7 red flowers, 7 yellow flowers, and 1 orange flower in a vase. How many flowers does Riley have in the vase in all?

_____ + _____ + _____ = _____

Riley has _____ flowers in the vase in all.

4. How many hands tall is the horse?

The horse is _____ hands tall.

5. 90 – 60 = _____

Page 9
Day 1: 5; Day 2: 23; Day 3:
3 + 2 = 5 pencils; Day 4: 6:00

Page 10
1. 5; 2. 25; 3. 4 + 2 = 6 fish; 4. 9:00;
5. 17

Page 11
Day 1: 9; **Day 2:** 5; **Day 3:** true;
Day 4: 7

Page 12
1. 10; 2. 14; 3. true; 4. 5; 5. 10

Page 13
Day 1: Answers will vary; **Day 2:**
3:00; **Day 3:** 8; **Day 4:** 6

Page 14
1. ; 2. 10:00; 3. 4; 4. 6; 5. 4

Page 15
Day 1: 8; **Day 2:** 20; **Day 3:** 15;
Day 4: false

Page 16
1. 15; 2. 19; 3. false; 4. 2; 5. true

Page 17
Day 1: 10, 6, 12; **Day 2:** 4 – 2 = 2, 2;
Day 3: 18; **Day 4:** 3 – 1 = 2

Page 18
1. 11, 3, 9; 2. 5 – 3 = 2, Two; 3. 13;
4. 6 – 1 = 5; 5. 13

Page 19
Day 1: 2, 3; **Day 2:** true; **Day 3:** 9;
Day 4: Answers will vary.

Page 20
1. 4, 10; 2. false; 3. 11; 4. true; 5. 4, 2

Page 21
Day 1: 8:30; **Day 2:** 18; **Day 3:** 8 – 4
= 4; **Day 4:** 9 – 3 = 6 apples

Page 22
1. 11 – 2 = 9, 9; 2. 11; 3. 12 – 3 = 9;
4. 18; 5. 2:30

Page 23
Day 1: 3, 2; **Day 2:** Check students' answers; **Day 3:** 13; **Day 4:** true

Page 24
1. 7, 8; 2. true; 3. 4; 4. Check students' answers; 5. 6

Page 25
Day 1: 16; **Day 2:** 18; **Day 3:** 3; **Day 4:** 7:30

Page 26
1. 12; 2. 5; 3. 16; 4. 11:00; 5. 7

Page 27
Day 1: Answers will vary; **Day 2:** 16, 8; **Day 3:** true; **Day 4:** 7

Page 28
1. 10; 2. true; 3. 11; 4. 15, 13; 5. true

Page 29
Day 1: 2; **Day 2:** 14; **Day 3:** 7, 10; **Day 4:** 6

Page 30
1. 1; 2. 9; 3. 16; 4. 7, 4; 5. 4

Page 31
Day 1: 1, 2, 3; **Day 2:** true; **Day 3:** 8; **Day 4:** Answers will vary but may include ▯▯▯▯ or ▭▭▭▭.

Page 32
1. 3, 2 1; 2. Answers will vary but may include ▨ or ▨; 3. 17; 4. false; 5. 11

Page 33
Day 1: Check students' answers; **Day 2:** 14; **Day 3:** Six; **Day 4:** 4

Page 34
1. 7; 2. 1; 3. Check students' answers; 4. 12; 5. 17

Page 35
Day 1: 18, 11; **Day 2:** 1, 2, 3; **Day 3:** Answers will vary but may include ▦ or ▦; **Day 4:** 13

Page 36

1. 16; 2. 1, 2, 3; 3. Answers will vary but may include or ; 4. 7; 5. 8, 12

Page 37

Day 1: 5; **Day 2:** 1; **Day 3:** 7; **Day 4:** Thirteen

Page 38

1. 4; 2. 4; 3. 1; 4. 5; 5. Nine

Page 39

Day 1: false; **Day 2:** Answers will vary but may include ; **Day 3:** 1, 2, 3; **Day 4:** 3, 8

Page 40

1. true; 2. 9, 9; 3. 1, 3, 2; 4. Answers will vary but may include ; 5. 0, 1

Page 41

Day 1: 8; **Day 2:** Check students' answers; **Day 3:** 3; **Day 4:** 7

Page 42

1. 18; 2. 4; 3. 2; 4. Check students' answers; 5. 6

Page 43

Day 1: Seven; **Day 2:** Fourteen; **Day 3:** 14, 2; **Day 4:** 2, 3, 1

Page 44

1. Six; 2. 8, 2; 3. 4; 4. 1, 2, 3; 5. Ten

Page 45

Day 1: 6; **Day 2:** 9, 19; **Day 3:** 11; **Day 4:** 8

Page 46

1. 10; 2. 16, 19; 3. 8; 4. 16, 12; 5. Seven

Page 47

Day 1: 3, 1, 2; **Day 2:** true; **Day 3:** 3; **Day 4:** Answers will vary but may include .

Page 48
1. Answers will vary but may include ⊕; 2. true; 3. 5; 4. false; 5. 1, 2, 3

Page 49
Day 1: 12; **Day 2:** 18; **Day 3:** 29; **Day 4:** 3, 2, 1

Page 50
1. 11; 2. 13; 3. 38; 4. 1, 3, 2; 5. 33

Page 51
Day 1: 2 tens, 1 one; **Day 2:** >; **Day 3:** 3; **Day 4:** 6

Page 52
1. 76; 2. >; 3. Three; 4. 16; 5. 1 ten, 5 ones

Page 53
Day 1: 16; **Day 2:** 2 tens, 8 ones; **Day 3:** <; **Day 4:** 29

Page 54
1. 1 ten, 9 ones; 2. <; 3. 15; 4. 25; 5. <

Page 55
Day 1: 2:00; **Day 2:** 42; **Day 3:** 6; **Day 4:** >

Page 56
1. 51; 2. 13; 3. Three; 4. >; 5. 5:30

Page 57
Day 1: Six; **Day 2:** 57; **Day 3:** Check students' answers; **Day 4:** 6 tens, 0 ones

Page 58
1. 69; 2. Check students' answers; 3. 3 tens, 0 ones; 4. 69; 5. Eleven

Page 59
Day 1: 2, 3, 1; **Day 2:** >; **Day 3:** 20; **Day 4:** 29

Page 60
1. <; 2. 7; 3. 33; 4. 2, 3, 1; 5. >

Page 61
Day 1: 3; **Day 2:** 8 tens and 0 ones;
Day 3: 6; **Day 4:** 50

Page 62
1. 4; 2. 4; 3. 40; 4. 12; 5. 4 tens and
0 ones

Page 63
Day 1: 6:30; **Day 2:** 55; **Day 3:** Five;
Day 4: <

Page 64
1. 9; 2. 72; 3. <; 4. 12:00; 5. 51

Page 65
Day 1: 18; **Day 2:** 88; **Day 3:** 4;
Day 4: 9 tens, 0 ones

Page 66
1. brown; 2. 5 tens, 0 ones;
3. 7 tens, 0 ones; 4. 18; 5. 95

Page 67
Day 1: 1 ten, 5 ones; **Day 2:** >;
Day 3: 5; **Day 4:** 73

Page 68
1. 11; 2. 53; 3. 1 ten, 1 one; 4. 11; 5. >

Page 69
Day 1: 5; **Day 2:** 6 + 6 + 4 = 16, 16;
Day 3: 59; **Day 4:** 7

Page 70
1. 7 + 4 + 2 = 13, 13; 2. 3; 3. 2; 4. 32;
5. 5 + 4 + 1 = 10, 10

Page 71
Day 1: Lynn; **Day 2:** 10; **Day 3:** 9;
Day 4: 16

Page 72
1. Five; 2. 8; 3. 7; 4. 16; 5. Two

Page 73
Day 1: 54; **Day 2:** 5 + 5 + 5 = 15, 15;
Day 3: 11; **Day 4:** 84

Page 74
1. 3 + 7 + 0 = 10, 10; 2. 86; 3. 1;
4. 7 + 2 + 6 = 15, 15; 5. 82

Page 75
Day 1: 16, 10; **Day 2:** 11:30;
Day 3: 20; **Day 4:** 73

Page 76
1. 40; 2. 4:00; 3. Eleven; 4. 10, 19;
5. 3:30

Page 77
Day 1: 6, 2; **Day 2:** 87; **Day 3:**
4 + 8 + 1 = 13, 13; **Day 4:** 5

Page 78
1. 88; 2. 6, 6; 3. 1 + 6 + 5 = 12, 12;
4. 5; 5. 2 + 5 + 1 = 8, 8

Page 79
Day 1: 13; **Day 2:** Check students'
answers; **Day 3:** 11; **Day 4:** 10

Page 80
1. 0; 2. Check students' answers;
3. 50; 4. 8; 5. 17

Page 81
Day 1: 7, 0; **Day 2:** 78; **Day 3:** 7;
Day 4: 3 + 3 + 5 = 11, 11

Page 82
1. 6 + 7 + 2 = 15, Fifteen; 2. 12; 3. 19;
4. 5 + 3 + 9 = 17, 17; 5. 18, 2

Page 83
Day 1: 14; **Day 2:** 2, Two; **Day 3:** 61;
Day 4: 0

Page 84
1. Two; 2. 50; 3. Eight; 4. 10; 5. 59

Page 85
Day 1: 8 + 7 + 2 = 17, 17; **Day 2:** 1;
Day 3: 6; **Day 4:** 68

Page 86
1. $6 + 3 + 1 = 10$, Ten; 2. 3; 3. 40;
4. 3; 5. $4 + 4 + 4 = 12$, 12

Page 87
Day 1: 50; **Day 2:** $7 + 5 + 3 = 15$, 15;
Day 3: 8; **Day 4:** 16

Page 88
1. 20; 2. 0; 3. $7 + 7 + 1 = 15$, 15; 4. 5;
5. 30